Who is J.K Rowling?

Tanya Turner

ISBN: 1500261416
ISBN-13: 978-1500261412

TABLE OF CONTENTS

J K Rowling – The Author of Magic

Introduction

Do you have a dream? Something so big it seems impossible? Some people dream about going to the moon. Well guess what; Neil Armstrong did! Some people dream about winning gold at the Olympics. Well guess what; Michael Phelps did! Some people dream about writing the best-selling children's book series in the world ever, which is turned into multi-million dollar movies. Well guess what; J K Rowling did!

Not only did J K Rowling achieve her dream but she did so through very difficult circumstances. Her mother had died and she was going through a divorce. She was left on her own with a baby to look after. She found herself in a strange new city without a job, or any hope. The only thing she had was an idea. That idea just happened to be Harry Potter!

In this report you will read about Joanne Rowling; the person behind the pen name J K Rowling. You will find out about her childhood, her school life, her time at university and the struggles in her young adult life. More importantly though, you will find out about how one woman with the odds stacked against her, became the richest author in the world.

CHAPTER 1: WHO IS JK ROWLING?

Why is she famous?

An image of JK Rowling with a Harry Potter and the Sorcerer's Stone on her lap.

JK Rowling is the author of the children's book series; Harry Potter. These books are so popular that they have sold over 450 million copies. They have been sold all over the world and translated into 70 different languages. Harry Potter has sold more books than any other book series in history!

Special edition Harry Potter books.

These very successful books were turned into movies. Like her books, they were also very popular. More people have seen the Harry Potter films than James Bond, Star Wars, Batman or Shrek. Her films became the biggest, most popular film series ever in history. The total amount of money made from all the movies put together is estimated at nearly 8 Billion Dollars. Rowling was very involved in the film making process. It was very important to her that the films followed the books as closely as possible and they maintained her vision throughout. Of course it also meant that she made a lot of money!

How successful is J K Rowling?

During the time that she was writing the first in the Harry Potter Series, her mother died, she was going through a divorce and had become very poor. She didn't give up writing though and after the amazing success of the Harry

Potter she is now estimated to have a fortune of $798 million!

J K Rowling has been recognized for many awards and achievements. In 2007, Forbes (an American business magazine) decided that she deserved to be the forty-eighth most powerful celebrity. In the same year another American magazine called TIME, said she was their runner up for their annual award called "Person of the Year". They made a point of highlighting that JK Rowling is a moral and social person with strong political opinions and that she had been an inspiration to her fans, young and old.

Her notoriety didn't stop there; in 2008 the UK magazine Sunday Times put Rowling on their annual rich list as the twelfth richest woman in Britain. In 2010 a group of top magazine editors decided that they were so impressed with Rowling's work and support of charities that they named her "The Most Influential Woman in Britain."

She is now known, not just as an author but as a philanthropist. This means that she is a person who has a lot of money but uses a fair amount of it to help people who are poor and needy. She has helped charities such as Comic Relief, One Parent Families, Lumos and the Multiple Sclerosis Society of Great Britain.

CHAPTER 2: LIFE BEFORE HARRY POTTER

The Early Years

JK Rowling was born on 31st July 1965. Her parents called their new little girl Joanne Rowling. Her mother was called Ann and her father was called Peter. She was born in a place in England called Yate.

Joanne has a younger sister called Dianne. There is less than two years between them. When she was four they moved to a village nearby called Winterbourne. It was there, when attending St Michaels Primary School that Joanne met the inspiration for Albus Dumbledore. The headmaster at this school was called Alfred Dunn. He was a kind, wise elderly head master that clearly left an impression on young Joanne.

Rowling always loved writing stories, even as a child. She would often read them to her little sister who would listen avidly. One of these stories was about a rabbit and a bee called "Rabbit and Miss Bee." Not the most original of name choices but she was only 5 years old at the time. In another story her sister was the heroine; in this tale her sister fell down a rabbit hole, just like in Alice in Wonderland. Joanne didn't totally copy the story of Alice though; in her version her sister was fed strawberries by the rabbit. It is interesting that Joanne's first few stories were about rabbits and we often associate rabbits with magic tricks. Maybe Rowling was always meant to write about a magical world!

She moved again when she was nine years old. Her family moved to a beautiful little English cottage called Church Cottage in the small Gloucestershire English village of Tutshill. This is where she lived while she was a teenager.

The Church Cottage at Tutshill, Gloucestershire, England where JK Rowling and her family used to live when she was just a teenager.

The Teenage Years

Joanne had a close relationship with her great aunt who encouraged her to study and to read. Rowling said her great aunt "…approved of a thirst for knowledge, even the questionable kind." She introduced Joanne to a book written by Jessica Mitford. This book was called Hons and Rebels. Joanne loved it and read all of Mitford's books. Mitford was a civil rights campaigner and a political activist. She had died before Joanne was even born but she was still a big inspiration to her.

When you think of the Harry Potter character; Hermione, you probably think of words such as bookish, know it all, geeky and clever. Well this was how Rowling would also describe herself at that age. She loosely based the Hermione character on herself, without all the witchy skills of course.

As an adult Joanne looks back on her teenage years with some level of sadness. She does not remember being happy at this time of her life. She went to Wydean School and College when she was eleven. Her school teacher, Steve Eddy taught her English and said that she was not exactly "exceptional." That is quite a surprise considering the success she now has using her English skills. He did concede that she was in a group of girls who were "quite good."

Actress Emma Watson as Hermione Granger, a character from Harry Potter books and movies where JK Rowling can relate herself when she was still a teenager.

After she did her compulsory exams at the age of 16 she went on to do her A levels in English, French and German. At this time, her best friend was a boy called Sean Harris. He owned a turquoise Ford Anglia. Fans of the book and film will know this car very well. It was the same kind that Harry and Ron flew to Hogwarts in when they missed the Hogwarts Express. The only difference being is that the Ford Anglia that belonged to Sean Harris probably didn't fly! Sean doesn't look like the character of Ron but Joanne has admitted that her school friend was her inspiration, saying that Ron is very "Seanish."

The turquoise flying Ford Anglia 105E Deluxe that was featured in the film Harry Potter and the Chamber of Secrets on display during Harry Potter The Exhibition at the Art Science Museum, Singapore.

During this time, her home life was quite unsettled. Her mother wasn't very well and her relationship with her father was challenging. Sadly the two of them no longer speak to each other.

Actor Rupert Grint as Ron Weasley, one of the main characters in the movie adaptation of Harry Potter series.

Like most teenagers, she loved music. The group she loved the most were called The Smiths, she also liked a band called The Clash. Both groups were very famous and popular at the time particularly with other British teenagers.

Life as a Young Adult

Joanne really wanted to go to Oxford University. This is one of the places that the really clever academic people in Britain go to study. It is very hard to get accepted though and she was not successful. Not deterred, in 1982, Rowling went to the University of Exeter to study French and the classics.

A part of the University of Exeter where JK Rowling study French.

She was hoping to go to university and meet other young people with "radical" left wing views like herself. It took some time to find these people, but once she did she settled in well and became very happy, enjoying university life.

Her professor of French remembered her as "a quietly competent student, with a denim jacket and dark hair, who in academic terms, gave the appearance of doing what was necessary."

In fact Joanne's own memory of her university days did not relate to academic work at all. She just remembers listening to music and wearing a lot of heavy eyeliner! To be fair she also remembers doing a lot reading, particularly works by Dickens and Tolkien. As part of the French element to her course she studied in Paris for a year.

Later, in 1998 Rowling wrote article about studying the classics at Exeter. They were very proud to have such a successful ex-student so they published it in their journal.

She graduated in 1986 and moved to London where she got a job as a researcher and bilingual secretary, bilingual means using two languages. This was the perfect job for Joanne as she was able to use her French and English skills at the same time. The company she was hired for was Amnesty International. This was brilliant for young Joanne because Amnesty International is an organization that helps people around the world. For many years Joanne had strongly believed in helping people and this job gave her an opportunity to work for the leading organization committed to doing just that.

CHAPTER 3: WRITING HARRY POTTER

The Birth of Harry

Rowling was stuck on a train, it was delayed and she had nothing to do. It was at this time, in this moment, that Harry Potter was born. She explains this pivotal moment in her life on her website;

"I was travelling back to London on my own on a crowded train, and the idea for Harry Potter simply fell into my head. I had been writing almost continuously since the age of six but I had never been so excited about an idea before. To my immense frustration, I didn't have a pen that worked, and I was too shy to ask anybody if I could borrow one… I did not have a functioning pen with me, but I do think that this was probably a good thing. I simply sat and thought, for four (delayed train) hours, while all the details bubbled up in my brain, and this scrawny, black-haired, bespectacled boy who didn't know he was a wizard became more and more real to me. Perhaps, if I had slowed down the ideas to capture them on paper, I might have stifled some of them (although sometimes I do wonder, idly, how much of what I imagined on that journey I had forgotten by the time I actually got my hands on a pen). I began to write 'Philosopher's Stone' that very evening, although those first few pages bear no resemblance to anything in the finished book."

Rowling started writing Harry Potter in 1990. It took seven years to complete the first book. In this time her life changed a great deal.

Actor Daniel Radcliffe as Harry Potter, the lead character in the movie adaptation of Harry Potter series.

Loss

Her mother died in the December of that year. She died of a disease called Multiple Sclerosis, which she had been very ill with for many years. Harry Potter's character also suffered loss; Joanne admits that she focused more on this factor of his life because her own mother had died.

Marriage and Divorce

Rowling got a job in Portugal teaching English as a foreign language in a night class. She carried on writing Harry Potter in the daytime while she listened to classical violin music for inspiration. It was there she met a television journalist from Portugal called Jorge Arantes. They got married in 1992 and had a little girl in 1993. Joanne wanted to name her daughter after her childhood heroine Jessica Witford, so they called her Jessica Isobel Rowling Arantas.

The marriage wasn't a happy one though, only 13 months after saying their vows, they separated. Rowling moved to Edinburgh in Scotland to be near her sister Diana. She had very little to call her own, but she did have three chapters of Harry Potter in her bag!

Overcoming Failure

It was this part of her life that Rowling describes as "rock bottom." She had no job, a failed marriage and was now a single parent. However, this didn't stop her from writing Harry Potter; in fact Harry was all she had. She has written about this time of her life since, in an article called "The Fringe Benefits of Failure."

"Failure meant a stripping away of the inessential. I stopped pretending to myself that I was anything other than what I was, and began to direct all my energy to finishing the only work that mattered to me. Had I really succeeded at anything else, I might never have found the determination to succeed in the one area - Harry Potter, in fact where I truly belonged. I was set free, because my greatest fear had been realized, and I was still alive, and I still had a daughter whom I adored, and I had an old typewriter, and a big idea. And so rock bottom became a solid foundation on which I rebuilt my life."

Even though Joanne can now look back on this difficult time and see the positives, back then, she didn't know how successful she would become. All the negativity in her life was too much and she became clinically depressed. This is a mental illness and sufferers feel as though all the happiness and joy in their life has been sucked out of them, as if their soul has been taken. Sound familiar? Typically of Rolwling, she turned a difficult situation into an inspiration. Following her depression, the Dementors were born.

There was a rumor for many years that she wrote in cafes so that she could get out of her unheated flat. She denies this, laughing it off because it is very cold in Scotland and it would not be very clever to live in a flat without heating! She did write in local cafes though, but her real reason was that her daughter would fall asleep in the pram on the way. It was true that money was a constant worry at this time; she described her situation as being "poor as it is possible to be in modern Britain without being homeless."

The Elephant Café, the coffee shop where JK Rowling spend time while writing the Harry Potter book.

Rowling was forced to apply for government benefits to support herself and her daughter. She didn't like being dependent on the state and decided she wanted to teach. She wasn't qualified to teach in Scotland and had to take a course which would take a year of full time study. In August 1995 she began her teaching qualification at Edinburgh University, just as she was finishing the first book.

CHAPTER 4: HARRY POTTERS JOURNEY TO SUCCESS

Getting Harry Published

Even though Harry Potter is now extremely successful, not everyone could see its potential. The first Harry Potter book was finished in 1995 and was called Harry Potter and the Philosopher's Stone. It was written on an old typewriter.

Rowling was lucky enough to get an agent, through Christopher Little Literary Agents. Their job was to help Rowling to get a publisher. Nobody seemed to want it though. After twelve rejections and a year of waiting, Bloomsbury Publishers gave her £1500 and agreed to print Harry Potter. It was the fantastic news that Joanne had been waiting over seven years to hear!

The decision went in Rowling's favor because of an eight year old girl. The chairman at this London based publishers, gave the first chapter to his daughter. As soon as she finished reading she wanted the next chapter. This made the chairman realize that this book might be special. However, he wasn't over confident; he did tell Rowling that despite his agreement to print the book he didn't believe she would make any money out of it. Luckily for Rowling she was awarded a special grant of £8000 from the Scottish Arts Council. This meant that she didn't need to get a day job and could just keep writing.

Harry Potter and the Philosopher's Stone

Finally in the spring of 1997 Harry Potter was published. Like many new books, only 1,000 were printed. People will now pay up to £25,000 for the pleasure of owning one of these first editions. They are particularly special because they are printed with the author's name as "Joanne Rowling." It was only after the first editions were published that Bloomsbury asked Joanne to create a pen name. They wanted a different name on the books because they were worried that young boys might be put off if they knew it was written by a girl. Joanne didn't have a middle name so she used K because her grandmother's name was Kathleen. This was how Joanne Rowling became J K Rowling.

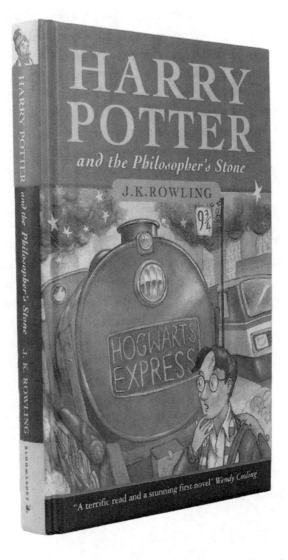

One of the first edition prints of JK Rowling's first Harry Potter book published by Bloomsbury with the original title, 'Harry Potter and the Philosopher's Stone'.

The book carried on growing in success and the name of J K Rowling became more famous. The first award it won was the Nestle Smarties Book Prize followed by the British Book Award for Children's Book of the Year. It later won the Children's Book Award.

In 1998, publishers in America were fighting over the book because they all wanted the rights to publish it. An auction was held and the big publishers Scholastic Inc won the contract for $105,000. Rowling was shocked by this news. She said she "nearly died."

Scholastic published the first Harry Potter book but it was renamed for American children. It was called Harry Potter and the Sorcerer's Stone. Rowling now says that this was a mistake and she wished she had made them stick to the original name. This made her determined to ensure she stayed more in control of the Harry Potter brand as the future progressed.

Joanne's life had completely changed within a very short period of time. She had gone from being an unpublished author on benefits to an award winning global author and this was still her first book. She was able to move out of her rented flat with her daughter and buy a new home for them. This must have been very exciting.

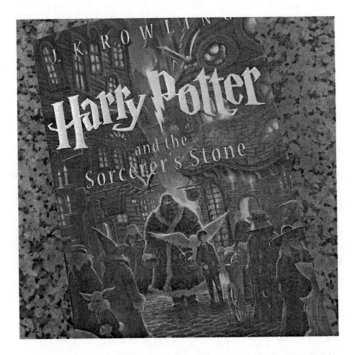

The US Version of JK Rowling's first Harry Potter book published by Scholastic Inc. with the title, 'Harry Potter and the Sorcerer's Stone.

The Sequels

There are eight books in the Harry Potter series. They are as follows:

- Harry Potter and the Philosopher's Stone – or Sorcerer's Stone in the US.

- Harry Potter and the Chamber of Secrets

- Harry Potter and the Prisoner of Azkaban

- Harry Potter and the Goblet of Fire

- Harry Potter and the Order of the Phoenix

- Harry Potter and the Half Blood Prince

- Harry Potter and the Deathly Hallows

The Chamber of Secrets

The first American edition of 'Harry Potter and the Chamber of Secrets'
published by Scholastic Inc.

It was nervous time for Rowling. Her first book was very successful and everyone was waiting for the next one with great excitement. It was no disappointment though, Harry Potter and the Chamber of Secrets was published in July 1998 and also won the Smarties award.

The Prisoner of Azkaban

A copy of JK Rowling's third Harry Potter book entitled 'Harry Potter and the Prisoner of Azkaban'.

The third in the series was published in December 1999 and was called Harry Potter and the Prisoner of Azkaban. This book won the Smarties award just like the others before it. No other book series had ever won the Smarties award three years in a row. The Prisoner of Azkaban also won the Whitbread Children's Book of the Year award. It was the same year that the new translated version of Beowulf came out though, and this book beat Harry Potter to the Book of the Year prize.

The Goblet of Fire

A copy of JK Rowling's fourth Harry Potter book entitled, 'Harry Potter and the Goblet of Fire'.

The forth book was called Harry Potter and the Goblet of Fire. It was the first in the series to be published in the UK and the US at the same time. Both came out in July 2000. By this time, so many people had read the first three books; they were waiting for this release and ready to buy it straight away. The result of this was that in the first 48 hours 372,775 copies were sold in the UK, breaking all previous records. In fact, that was almost the same number of books that the third book sold in its first year. The US book sales were also impressive with 3 million books sold in those same 48 hours.

Writing this book was the biggest challenge for Rowling since she began writing about Harry. She kept it to herself at the time but has since admitted that she really struggled in the writing process. She rewrote one chapter 13 times, but no one has been able to work out which one and she refuses to tell. Rowling has proved very good at keeping secrets.

The Order of the Phoenix

A copy of JK Rowling's fifth Harry Potter book enttled, 'Harry Potter and the Order of the Phoenix'.

The first four books came quickly after each other, but the fans had to wait three years for the fifth; Harry Potter and the Order of the Phoenix was released in 2003. Lots of people were saying Rowling must have had writers block, which is when a writer just loses ideas. Rowling kept denying it and later said that she simply found this book "a chore." She wishes now that it was shorter because she felt she had no energy left by the time she had finished.

The Half Blood Prince

A copy of JK Rowling's sixth Harry Potter book entitled, 'Harry Potter and the Half-blood Prince'.

The fans were far from bored with Harry Potter. In July 2005 the Half-Blood Prince was released and broke previous Harry Potter sales records. It sold nine million copies in only 24 hours. When talking about writing book six she explained that she had already planned the storyline of book six years previously. As a writer though the story often changes from what you originally planned. An example of this is the first chapter of this book; the British Prime Minister and the Minister of Magic have a conversation. Rowling wanted this in the first book, and then the second and then the third before she finally decided it really belonged in the Half-Blood Prince. This sixth book received the Book of the Year prize at the British Book Awards.

The Deathly Hallows

A copy and the seventh and last book of the Harry Potter series entitled, 'Harry Potter and the Deathly Hallows'.

By the time the seventh was due out the fan base was global and enormous. People just couldn't wait. It became a massive news story in December when it was announced that the title of the book was going to be Harry Potter and the Deathly Hallows. At this point, Rowling was still writing it! Joanne was staying in the Balmoral Hotel in Edinburgh and wrote on a bust that she had finished it. She didn't get into trouble though; the hotel was very happy and now makes sure all the guests know about the special J K Rowling graffiti!

The book was released in July 2007. It sold even faster than all the others put together. People camped out all night to get the first copies. 11 million books were sold in the first day in the UK and the US.

Rowling had the entire storyline and plot planned years before; in fact she had written the last chapter of the last book at the same time she had written the first few of the Philosopher's Stone, 17 years before its release.

As she was finishing this last book she was filmed by a BBC crew for a documentary. They took her back to the flat that she lived with her daughter after the divorce. Joanne ended up in tears; she said it was "where I turned my life around completely."

CHAPTER 5: THE HARRY POTTER MOVIES

The Journey to Hollywood

Warner Bros bought the rights for the first two books. The first adaptation came to the cinema screens of expectant fans in 2001 and the sequel, The Chamber of Secrets was released soon after in 2002. After these two proved to be hugely successful the rest of the books were given the go ahead. It was a two year wait for Prisoner of Azkaban but only another year till Goblet of Fire. After another two year wait the Order of the Phoenix was released in 2007. The film makers were keen to catch up with the books to keep up with the hype. Harry Potter films, books and merchandise were everywhere. It was as if Harry Potter was taking over the world!

The Warner Brothers logo. The company that bought the rights of all seven Harry Potter books for movie adaptation.

The last book had a lot of information to cover and the film makers, along with Rowling, felt it would be too much to show in just one film. They therefore made the decision to create two. The Deathly Hallows part 1 was released in 2010 and part 2 followed in 2011.

Rowling's Role in the Films

It is very rare that films follow books exactly. It was very important to Rowling that she had an active role and was able to work directly with the script writers to ensure that the true vision of Harry Potter was kept alive.

It was also important because when Warner Bros started to make the films, the books series hadn't finished. Joanne admitted that she shared some of the storyline secrets with the main script writer and even a few of the characters. It was important that the scriptwriters were in the loop so that they didn't write anything into the film that wouldn't fit into the future storylines. She wanted to share with some of the secrets with the actors so that they could gain a deeper understanding into their characters actions and then play them better. She did not share all of the secrets about Harry Potter with anyone though. This way she remained in control at all times.

With her charity work now an important part of her life, Rowling insisted that Coca-Cola donate $18 million to an American organization called "Reading is Fundamental." She also insisted that the film was entirely filmed in Britain and at all possible times had British actors. Warner Bros did everything they could to keep Rowling happy.

It was originally discussed that Joanne should appear in the film as the ghostly Lily Potter. You can see a resemblance in the woman, Geraldine Somerville that eventually took the job. Joanne just couldn't face the thought of acting; despite it only being a small part she was sure she would "mess everything up!"

At the British Academy Film Awards it won the prize for Outstanding British Contribution to Cinema in 2011. This is one of the biggest prizes in the British film making industry.

CHAPTER 6: LIFE AFTER HARRY

Fame and Fortune

JK Rowling was the first author to become a billionaire. She isn't a billionaire anymore though because she gives so much money to charity.

She isn't shy of getting involved and sharing her opinions on politics. Usually when she does it has something to do with helping children who are poor.

She now lives in a big estate house looking over the river Tay, still in Scotland. She also owns a house in a very expensive area in the center of London and another on the capitals outskirts.

Family Life

After her first divorce, she had not been put off marriage entirely. In 2001 she married a doctor called Neil Murray. They had a baby boy called David in 2003 and another daughter called Mackenzie born in 2005. All of her 3 children have been born while she was writing Harry Potter even though there was a 12 year gap between her oldest and youngest.

Joanne has always had a difficult relationship with her dad. But she hasn't spoken to him at all since 2003. One of the reasons she gave for this was that her father had sold a special copy of a Harry Potter book she had given him and signed personally for father's day. Her father sold the book for £50.000 but lost his daughter in the process.

CHAPTER 7: WRITING SINCE HARRY

The Casual Vacancy

In 2012 JK Rowling published a new book called the Casual Vacancy. This was her first book aimed at adults. It sold over a million copies and is being made into a television show which will be on the BBC in 2014.

A copy of JK Rowling's 'The Casual Vacancy', an adult book published by Little, Brown Book Group.

What's next?

JK Rowling has done several interviews over the last few years and people will always ask her about her up and coming books. The answers that she tends to give do vary which suggests that she is either keeping secrets (which we know she is good at as she held on to the secrets of Harry Potter for 17 years) or maybe she is not sure herself. After all, Harry Potter has been such a big part of her life it would definitely be hard to separate yourself from something that big.

She has said that she doesn't feel she should write any more fantasy. She created such an amazing, detailed and intricate world of wizards, witches, giants and magic that if she was to try to create another fantasy world she would be worried that it would end up overlapping with Harry's.

She has been talking about a children's story about a monster called a "Political Fairy" for several years. Fans are still eagerly waiting. She has also mentioned that she is still writing for adults. However she has stated that she prefers writing for children.

She is so famous; anything that she does publish is bound to be successful. People also have very high expectations and this puts a lot of pressure on her as an author. This is why she has said that she would like to write under a fake name. This way her work would be judged fairly on its merit alone, but she thinks the press would find out quickly anyway and so there would be no point.

What about Harry?

Rowling thinks it is "very unlikely" that there will be another Harry Potter book, but she refuses to say never. She did have plans to publish a highly illustrated encyclopedia with all the different terms and definitions of Harry's world along with unpublished material she has written in the past. If it is ever published, all the money is supposed to go to charity.

Since talking about this though she has since launched a new website called Potterworld. This is a space where she has published 18.000 words for free. The most recent time she was asked about the encyclopedia she said that she was enjoying giving the fans an opportunity to access this information for free.

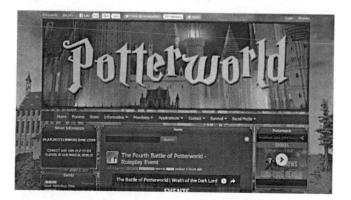

Homepage of the Potterworld website (www.potterworldmc.com), where JK Rowling published words used in her Harry Potter book series.

CHAPTER 8: WHAT CAN WE LEARN FROM J K ROWLING?

Never Give Up!

Joanne faced some major difficulties in her life while she was trying to write the first Harry Potter book. She took the negative situations in her life, like her divorce, her mother's death, her depression and instead of letting these things get her down; she used them to help her writing.

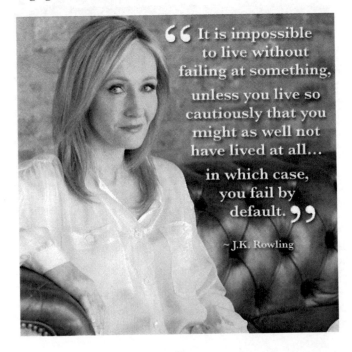

It is impossible to live without failing at something, unless you live so cautiously that you might as well not have lived at all... in which case, you fail by default.

~ J.K. Rowling

A very inspiring quote from JK Rowling.

When she was in school or at university she wasn't the most amazing student, her teachers didn't know she would become a writing superstar. She was clearly talented but more than anything she was determined. If we can learn anything from Joanne Rowling it is if you have a dream, don't just chase it, catch it!

ABOUT THE AUTHOR

Tanya Turner is a sixth grade teacher. She enjoys writing, and spends time daily writing a blog, paper journals, and reports. She also loves reading and doing researches. Tanya Turner is also a mom to a 15-month old cute and loveable baby: Uno. She has been married to her husband, Matthew, for 4 years. She is a sister too with one brothers and two sisters. In her free time, sleeping, reading, riding her bike, hiking in nature, eating and travelling are Tanya's pastimes. Also, Tanya looks forward to reading many books, writing often, and developing her own interest and skill at writing.

*Images from: Daniel Ogren, darth_martus, Ghmyrtle, orionpozo,
Jack at Wikipedia, 金妮• ㄚ ㄚ, Benjamin Evans, Dave
Catchpole, Tom Marble, AbeBooks, Ray Bouknight,
BrokenSphere, Shannon, ;Deirdreamer, Sonia Belviso, Matthew
Bloomfield, woodleywonderworks, Insomnia Cured Here, Gwydion
M. Williams, Walter Lim/Flicker/Wikimedia Commons*

CPSIA information can be obtained
at www.ICGtesting.com
Printed in the USA
LVOW10s0916250617
539310LV00012B/345/P